A+ books

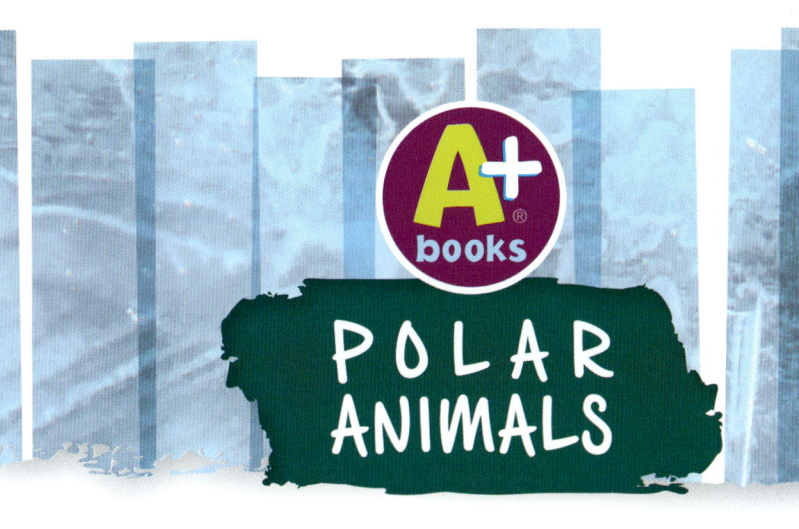

POLAR ANIMALS

KILLER WHALES
ARE AWESOME

Jaclyn Jaycox

raintree
a Capstone company — publishers for children

Raintree is an imprint of Capstone Global Library Limited, a company incorporated in England and Wales having its registered office at 264 Banbury Road, Oxford, OX2 7DY – Registered company number: 6695582

www.raintree.co.uk
myorders@raintree.co.uk

Text © Capstone Global Library Limited 2020
The moral rights of the proprietor have been asserted.

All rights reserved. No part of this publication may be reproduced in any form or by any means (including photocopying or storing it in any medium by electronic means and whether or not transiently or incidentally to some other use of this publication) without the written permission of the copyright owner, except in accordance with the provisions of the Copyright, Designs and Patents Act 1988 or under the terms of a licence issued by the Copyright Licensing Agency, Barnard's Inn, 86 Fetter Lane, London, EC4A 1EN (www.cla.co.uk). Applications for the copyright owner's written permission should be addressed to the publisher.

Edited by Nikki Potts
Designed by Kayla Rossow
Picture research by Morgan Walters
Production by Laura Manthe
Originated by Capstone Global Library Limited
Printed and bound in India

ISBN 978 1 4747 8627 0 (hardback)
ISBN 978 1 4747 8639 3 (paperback)

British Library Cataloguing in Publication Data
A full catalogue record for this book is available from the British Library

Acknowledgements
We would like to thank the following for permission to reproduce photographs: Getty Images: VALERY HACHE, spread 20; Newscom: Galen Rowell/Mountain Light, 10, Gerard Lacz/agefotostock, 23, Rod Harbinson/Polaris, 25; Shutterstock: Alessandro De Maddalena, spread 26, AnnstasAg, (whale) 19, (fish) 19, Damian Palus, 24, DCrane, 12, Foto 4440, spread 15-16, Igor Kruglikov, 9, Inger Eriksen, 29, Martens Tom, 22, Michael Ferrell, 11, Rich Carey, top 27, robert mcgillivray, spread 18-19, Sebastian Kaulitzki, 7, Tatiana Ivkovich, 4, 5, Tory Kallman, Cover, 13, 16, TOSP, 6, vladsilver, 17, wildestanimal, 8, 28.

We would like to thank Greg Breed, Associate Professor of Ecology at the Institute of Arctic Biology, University of Alaska, for his invaluable help in the preparation of this book.

Every effort has been made to contact copyright holders of material reproduced in this book. Any omissions will be rectified in subsequent printings if notice is given to the publisher.

All the internet addresses (URLs) given in this book were valid at the time of going to press. However, due to the dynamic nature of the internet, some addresses may have changed, or sites may have changed or ceased to exist since publication. While the author and publisher regret any inconvenience this may cause readers, no responsibility for any such changes can be accepted by either the author or the publisher.

CONTENTS

Amazing killer whales 4

Hidden enemy 6

On the hunt 14

Family life 20

Staying safe 24

Glossary 30

Find out more 31

Websites 31

Comprehension questions 32

Index 32

Amazing killer whales

A killer whale explodes out of the water. A huge wave splashes up. The killer whale crashes back into the sea. *Splash!*

These playful marine mammals are also known as orcas. Despite their name, killer whales are not actually whales! They are the largest type of dolphin.

Hidden enemy

Killer whales are black and white. Their colour makes them hard to see. From below, their white stomachs look like the sky. Fish swimming underneath might not see them until it's too late.

Chomp! Killer whales have about 50 cone-shaped teeth. These help them to bite and tear prey.

7

Killer whales can weigh up to 10 tons. Male killer whales can be up to 10 metres (33 feet) long. That's nearly the length of a bus!

flukes

pectoral fin

dorsal fin

A tall dorsal fin sticks up from a killer whale's back. Killer whales flap the flukes on their tails to help them swim. Their pectoral fins help them steer.

Killer whales live in every ocean. They spend time in deep and shallow water. Killer whales are found in cold Antarctic and sub-Arctic waters. They also spend time in warm waters.

Killer whales have a thick layer of fat called blubber. It keeps them warm in the icy, polar water.

Killer whales move slowly through the water. They stay near the surface to breathe air through a blowhole on the top of their head.

Killer whales sleep with one eye open. The open eye watches for danger.

On the hunt

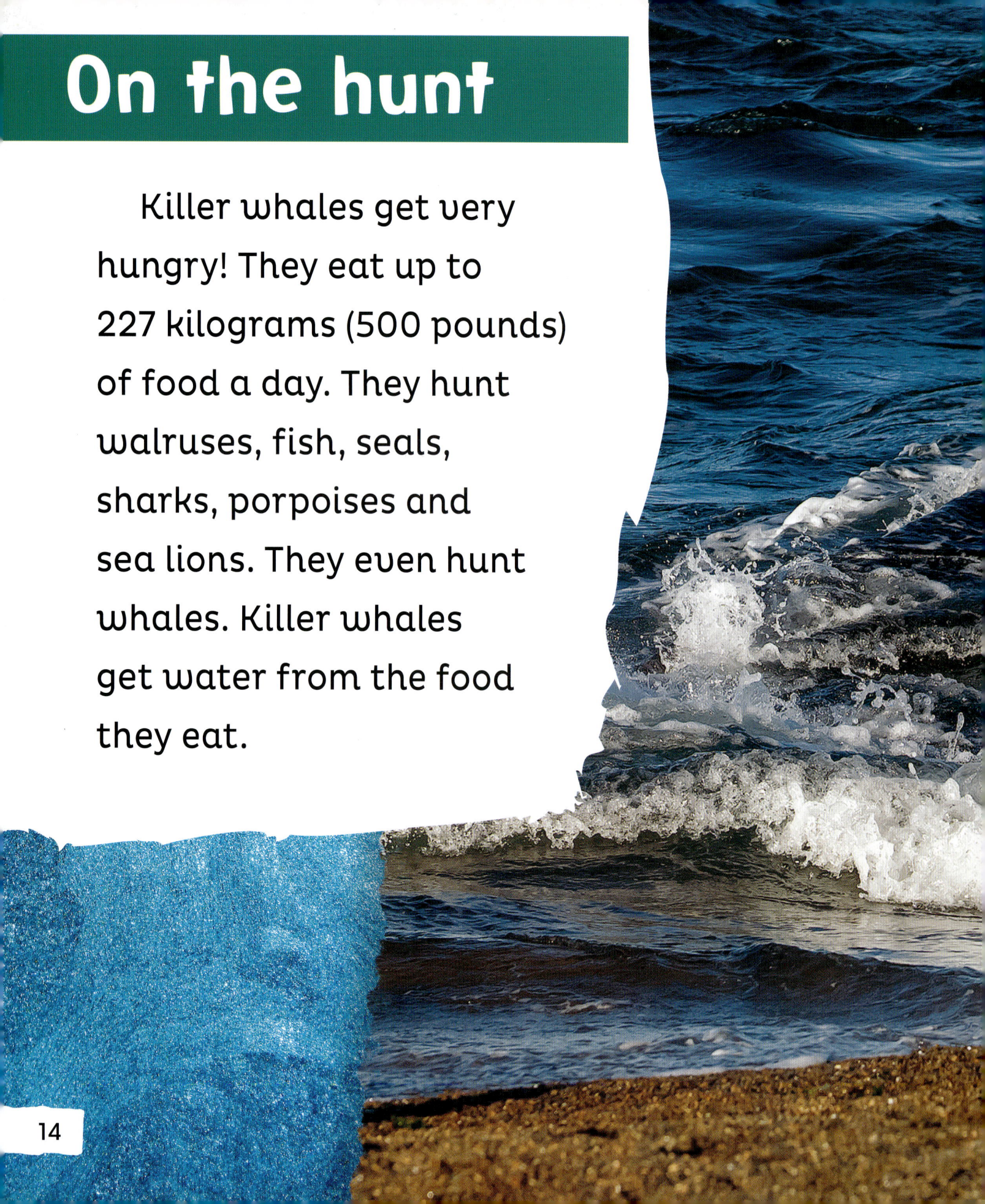

Killer whales get very hungry! They eat up to 227 kilograms (500 pounds) of food a day. They hunt walruses, fish, seals, sharks, porpoises and sea lions. They even hunt whales. Killer whales get water from the food they eat.

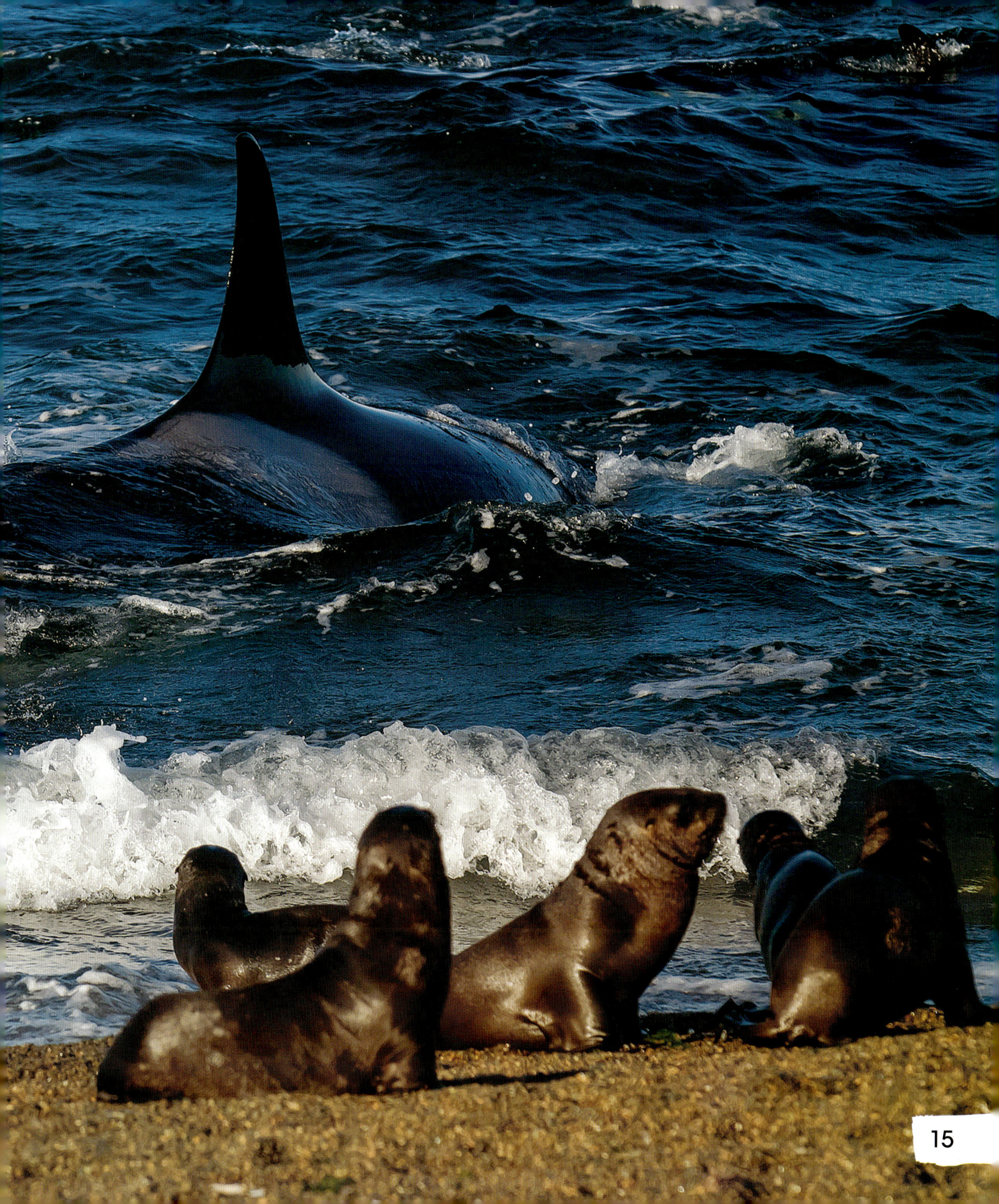

Killer whales hunt together in groups called pods. Pods can have up to 40 killer whales in them.

A seal sits on a floating piece of ice. Each killer whale in the pod takes turns making big waves. *Splash!* The seal is pushed into the water. The pod has caught its prey.

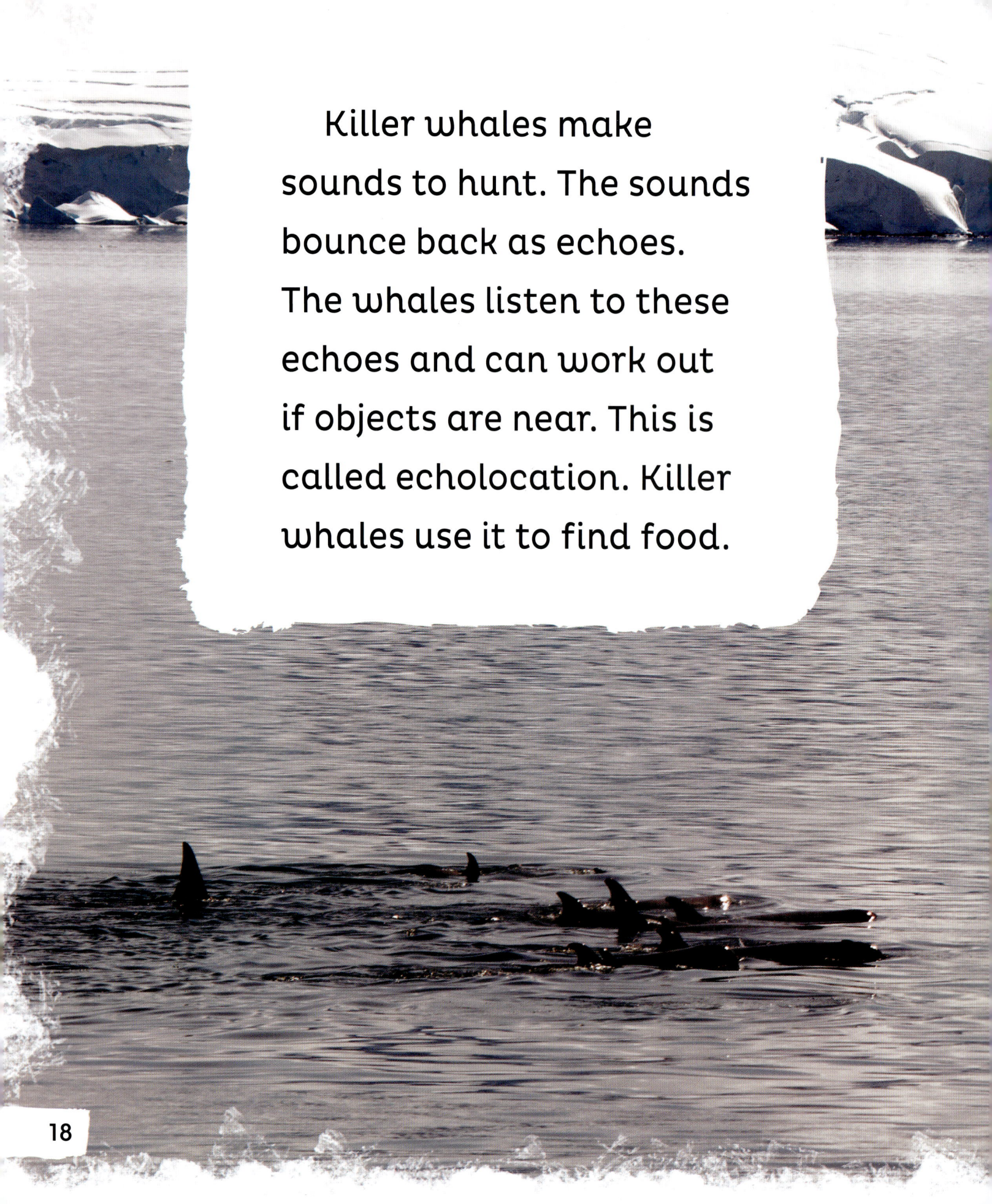

Killer whales make sounds to hunt. The sounds bounce back as echoes. The whales listen to these echoes and can work out if objects are near. This is called echolocation. Killer whales use it to find food.

Killer whales also communicate with each other using sounds. They click and whistle. A whale can hear its pod from miles away.

sound waves

Family life

Female killer whales give birth about every five years. A baby killer whale is called a calf. One calf is born at a time.

At birth, a calf weighs about 180 kilograms (400 pounds). The fin on a calf's back is floppy at first.

A calf drinks milk from its mother. Milk helps the calf grow blubber. The pod teaches the calf how to hunt and stay safe.

Most killer whales stay with their mothers all their lives. Killer whales live for about 50 years.

Staying safe

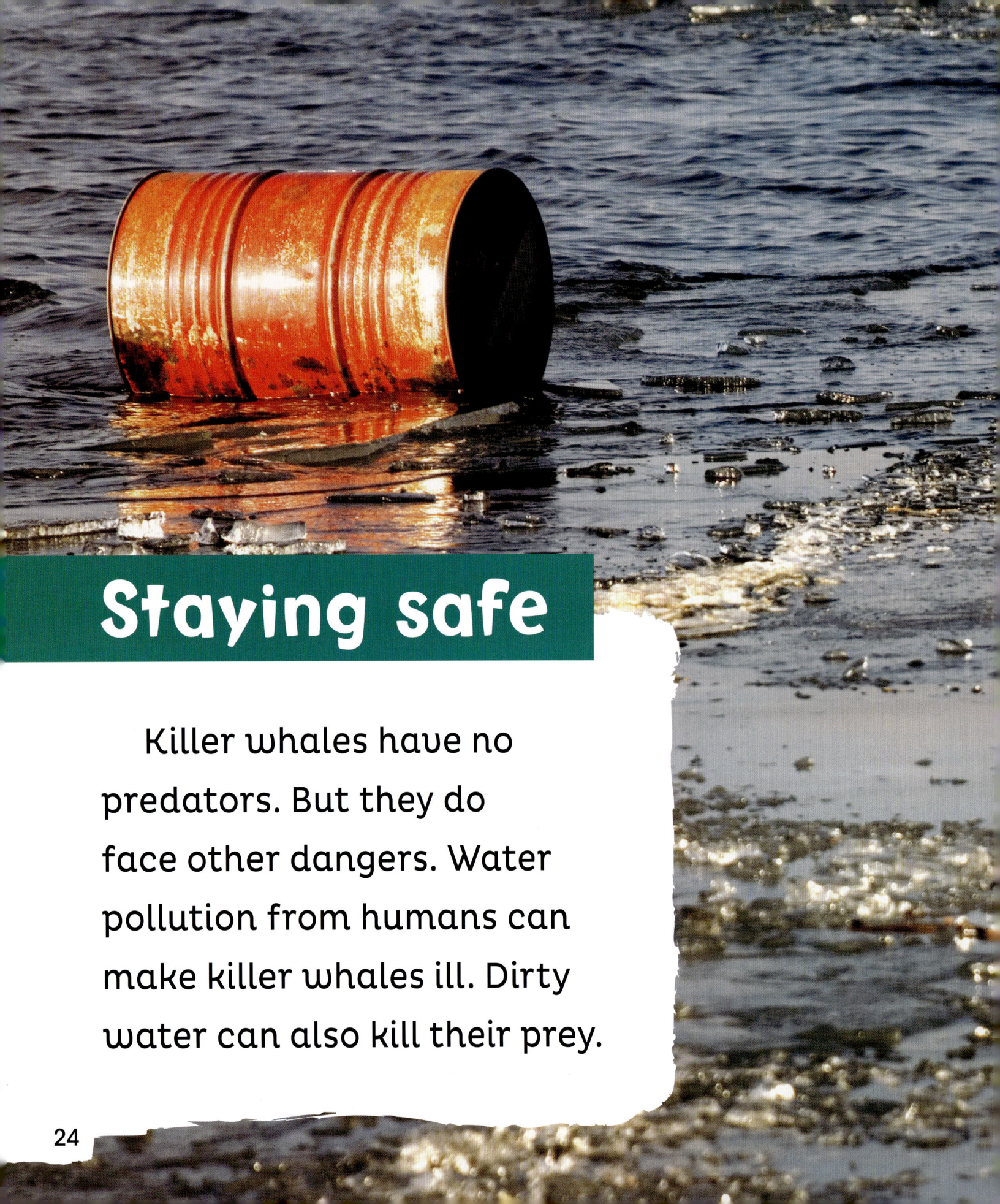

Killer whales have no predators. But they do face other dangers. Water pollution from humans can make killer whales ill. Dirty water can also kill their prey.

People sometimes catch too many fish. With less fish in the oceans, some killer whales could find it hard to get enough food.

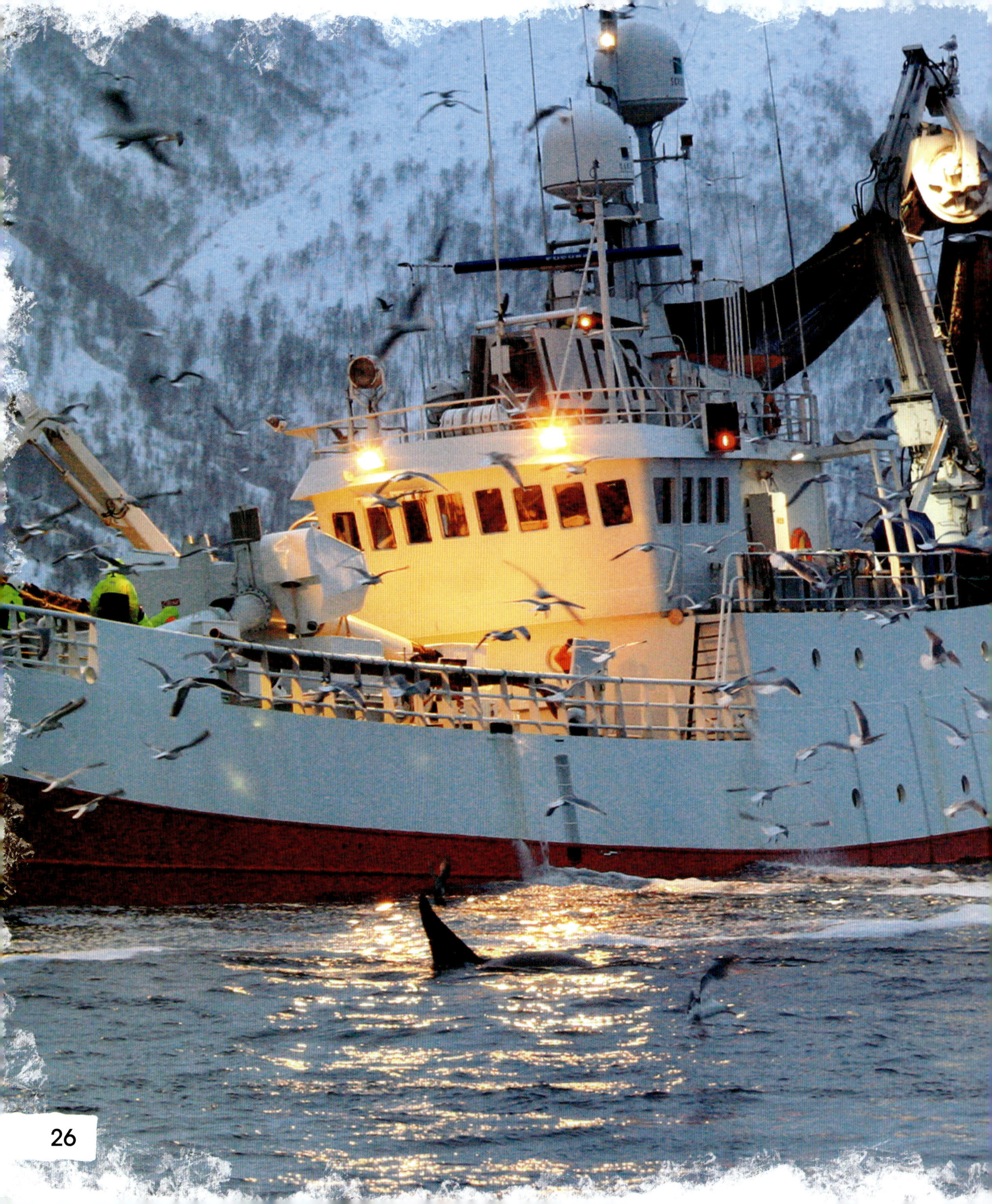

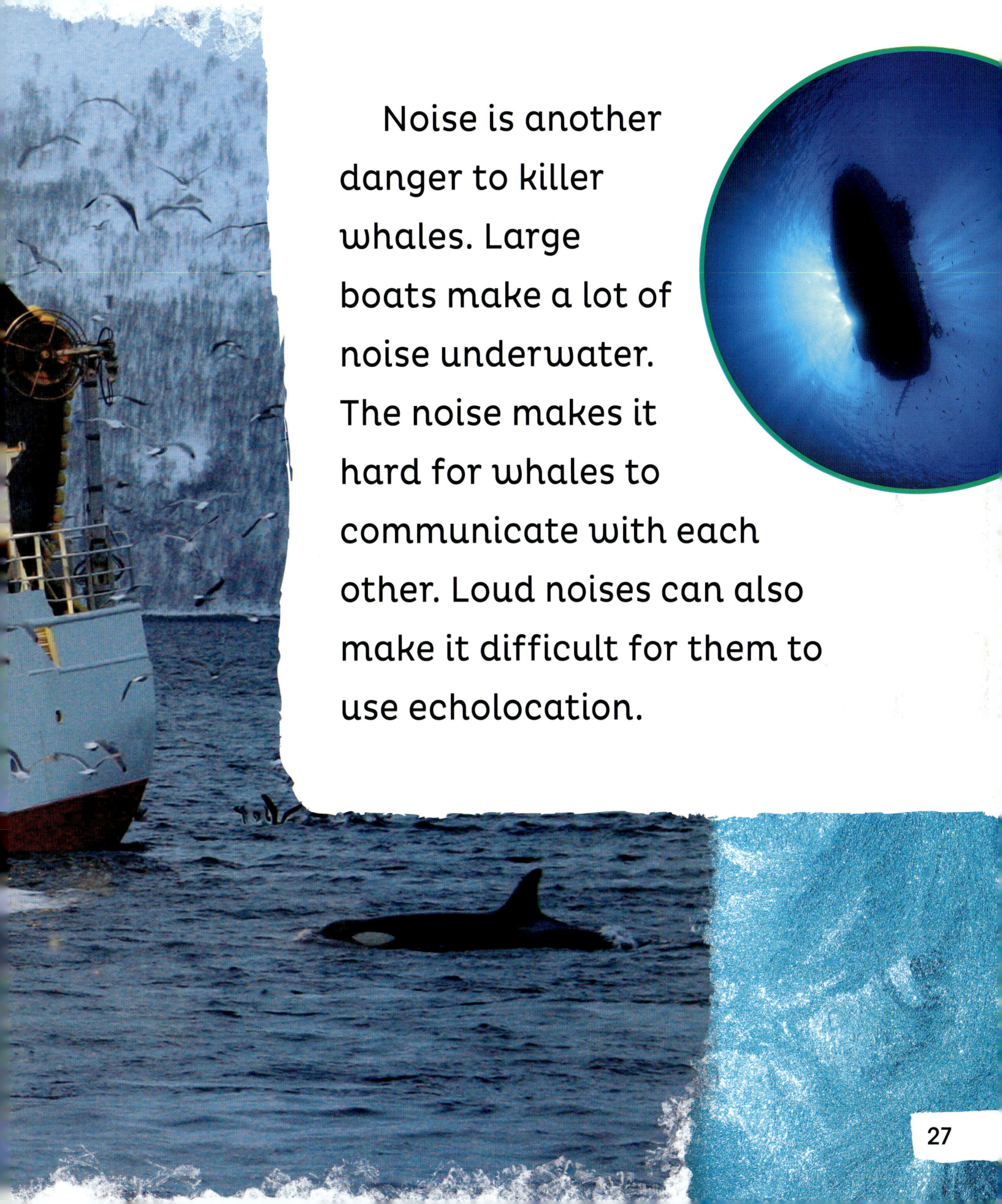

Noise is another danger to killer whales. Large boats make a lot of noise underwater. The noise makes it hard for whales to communicate with each other. Loud noises can also make it difficult for them to use echolocation.

Killer whales are one of the world's top predators. These beautiful, powerful dolphins spend their whole lives with their families.

Pods work together to hunt and raise young. These amazing polar animals depend on each other for survival.

GLOSSARY

Arctic area near the North Pole; the Arctic is cold and covered with ice

blowhole hole on the top of a whale's head; whales breathe air through blowholes

blubber thick layer of fat under the skin of some animals; blubber keeps animals warm

dorsal fin fin located on the back

echolocation process of using sounds and echoes to locate objects; whales and dolphins use echolocation to find food

female animal that can give birth to young animals or lay eggs

fluke wide, flat area at the end of a killer whale's tail; killer whales move their flukes to swim

habitat natural place and conditions in which a plant or animal lives

mammal warm-blooded animal that breathes air; female mammals feed milk to their young

pectoral fin one of a pair of fins found on the side of a whale's body

pod group of certain kinds of sea creatures

polar to do with the icy regions around the North or South Pole

pollution materials that hurt the Earth's water, air and land

predator animal that hunts other animals for food

prey animal hunted by another animal for food

surface top layer of something

FIND OUT MORE

Killer Whales (Nature's Children), Charnan Simon (Children's Press, 2012)

Killer Whales Are Not Whales! (Confusing Creature Names), Daisy Alynn (Gareth Stevens Publishing, 2014)

Orcas (Animal Abilities), Anna Claybourne (Raintree, 2013)

Shark vs. Killer Whale (Animal Rivals), Isabel Thomas (Raintree, 2017)

WEBSITES

Active Wild, Killer Whale Facts
www.activewild.com/killer-whale-facts-for-kids/

Animal Fact Guide
animalfactguide.com/animal-facts/killer-whale/

National Geographic, Orca
www.nationalgeographic.com/animals/mammals/o/orca/

COMPREHENSION QUESTIONS

1. Water pollution is one thing that can harm killer whales. What is pollution? (Hint: use the glossary for help!)

2. Where do killer whales live?

3. How do killer whales stay warm?

INDEX

Antarctic 10
Arctic 10
blowholes 12
blubber 11, 22
calves 20, 21, 22
dangers 13, 24, 27
dolphins 5, 28
echolocation 18
eyes 13
fins 9, 21

flukes 9
food 6, 14, 17, 18, 22, 24, 25, 27
orcas 5
pods 16, 17, 19, 22, 29
size 8, 21
sounds 18, 19, 27
stomachs 6
tails 9
teeth 6